DATE DUE

Daphne

A Trumpeter Swan

by
Bonnie Highsmith Taylor

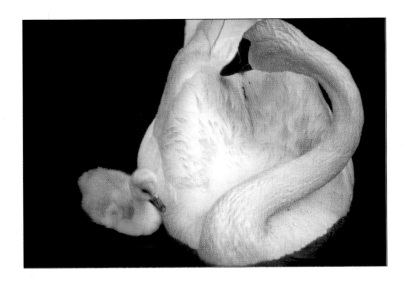

Perfection Learning®

Dedication

For my writer friend, Irene Bennett Brown

About the Author

Bonnie Highsmith Taylor is a native Oregonian. She loves camping in the Oregon mountains and watching birds and other wildlife. Writing is Ms. Taylor's first love. But she also enjoys going to plays and concerts, collecting antique dolls, and listening to good music.

Ms. Taylor is the author of several Animal Adventures books, including *Kip: A Sea Otter* and *Roscoe: A North American Moose.*

Cover Photo: Windland Rice (www.jfoott.com)

Image Credits: Jeff Foott (www.jfoott.com) pp. title page, 6–7, 11, 13, 16, 17, 20, 27, 28–29, 30, 34, 42, 45, 48, 50, 53; Windland Rice pp. 5, 8, 10, 12, 14–15, 18, 22, 24, 35, 39, 43, 47; EyeWire p. 19

Corel Professional Photos pp. 25, 26, 31, 36, 37, 40, 49; Digital Stock p. 44; some images copyright www.arttoday.com

Printed in the United States of America. For information, contact Perfection Learning® Corporation, 1000 North Second Avenue, P.O. Box 500, Logan, Iowa 51546-0500.
Tel: 1-800-831-4190 • Fax: 1-712-644-2392

Paperback ISBN 0-7891-5156-1
Cover Craft® ISBN 0-7807-9312-9

4

Contents

Chapter 1

It was almost the first of May. Snow had melted around the pond. Green shoots of grass and plants were growing. Spring lilacs and marsh marigolds were blooming.

Pond snails had laid their eggs on water plants. Hundreds of eggs sat on each leaf. When the babies hatched, they would eat the leaves.

Overhead, a pair of huge white birds circled. They were trumpeter swans. And they were looking for a place to nest.

It would be the female's, or *pen's*, first year to lay eggs. Daphne was four years old. The male, or *cob*, was also four years old.

They had met a year ago. Daphne and her mate would stay together for the rest of their lives. But now, it was time for them to start their first family.

They were returning from their winter feeding area. Would there be a good place on the pond to nest?

It would have to be a safe place. It couldn't be a place predators could reach easily. And there would have to be plenty of food nearby.

Trumpeter swans eat lots of plants. These plants grow in and near the water. Sago pondweed, duck potatoes, and other plants are some favorites. Swans eat the leaves, stems, and seeds.

All winter, Daphne and her mate had fed in farmers' fields. Other swans and geese had been there too. They had feasted on vegetables left after harvest. When the vegetables were gone, the birds ate grass.

One swan can eat up to ten pounds of grass a day. This is about one-third of a swan's weight. Adult trumpeters can weigh up to 30 pounds.

Swans have large, powerful wings. Their wingspan can be up to eight feet. Adult swans can actually beat large animals or humans to death with their wings.

Daphne and her mate circled the pond. Below, they saw a muskrat house. Swans often make their nests on top of muskrat or beaver homes.

After circling a few more minutes, the pair
landed. They walked around and around. They
were tired after their long flight.

Daphne stood on one leg. She stretched the
other. Then she stood on the other leg,
stretching the opposite one. Her mate did the
same.

They fed on the plants beside the pond.
They were very hungry. But they were more
tired than hungry.

The sun was sinking low. Songbirds flew to their roosting places and nests. Small animals crawled into holes in the ground and in trees.

Daphne and her mate preened their feathers. Then they lay down in the tall grass at the edge of the pond.

Trumpeter swan preening

Daphne and her mate stretched their long necks across their backs. Then they tucked their bills under their wings. They slept soundly.

Frogs croaked. An owl
hooted from a tall fir tree. In
the distance, a coyote
howled.

Daphne's mate stretched
out his long neck. He
answered the howl of the
coyote. For over a mile, the
sound echoed in the darkness.

Chapter 2

Daphne and the cob woke at daybreak. They were hungry. They paddled across the pond.

Now and then, they ducked their heads beneath the water. They pulled up plants to eat. They also fed on duckweed that floated

on top of the water. The swans skimmed the
water with their bills. As they did, they
swallowed green algae.

Feeding on the bottom of lakes and ponds
can be dangerous. People often drop lead
sinkers in the water. The sinkers are used for
fishing. But they can be deadly to swans and
other wildlife that swallow them.

Waterbirds also swallow lead-shot pellets from shotguns. These are dropped by hunters. One or two pellets are enough to kill a swan.

Daphne and her mate fed for some time. Then they searched for a good nesting site.

On the other side, a moose waded in the pond. She put her head down into the water. She brought up a mouthful of plants from the bottom. In the tall grass at the edge of the pond, her new calf lay hidden.

The swans watched the moose for a while. She was no threat to them. A long-legged heron feeding on small fish and tadpoles was no threat either. Neither were the ducks on the pond.

The trumpeters swam around the muskrat house. It looked like a good nesting place. But then, Daphne spotted a small island. It was about 20 feet from the bank.

She swam to it. The cob followed her. They walked around the small island. They looked it over carefully. Sedges and cattails grew there.

Trumpeter swa

Swans have few enemies. Sometimes raccoons, owls, or eagles steal swans' eggs. Or they might kill the young, called *cygnets*. But this doesn't happen often. Adult swans are very good at defending their young and themselves.

Humans can be enemies too. Trumpeter swans are protected by law. But even so, some are killed illegally. They are often mistaken for tundra swans. Tundra swans are legal game in some places.

Trumpeters are much larger than tundra and mute swans. Trumpeter swans are the largest waterfowl in North America. And they are the largest swans in the world.

Tundra swan

The snow-white trumpeter swans have black bills, feet, and legs. They have a thin reddish orange line on the lower part of their bills.

Trumpeters make very unusual sounds. Their loud calls sound like KO-HO, KO-HO. The calls can be heard for miles. Because of their calls, Native Americans called trumpeter swans *Ko-ho*.

These swans were named for their long windpipes. They are coiled like trumpets. The windpipes wind from their lungs to the breastbone to the throat.

Tundra swans were once called *whistling swans*. They are also snow-white. They have black bills with a small yellow mark in front of their eyes.

Mute swans are white. Their bills are pink or orange. They swim with their necks in an S-curve. They hold their wings slightly raised over their backs.

Mute swan

Mute swans are not really mute. But they don't have the same vocal systems that other swans have. They make hissing and snorting sounds.

Tundra and trumpeter swans fly without making any noise. But when mute swans fly, their wings make deep humming or buzzing sounds.

All young swans are brownish gray until after they are a year old. Sometimes they are this color even longer.

At last, Daphne decided the small island would be a good place to raise her family. First she and her mate had to build a nest. It would take about two weeks.

The island was only about eight feet across. The nest would be at least six feet across.

Daphne lay down in the middle of the island. She stretched out her long neck. She gathered all the grass and sedge she could reach. She packed it all around her body.

The cob swam across the pond. On the bank, he gathered cattails and reeds. He swam back to the nest with them.

Daphne arranged them in a large circle. The pair worked for an hour to two.

Then they paddled around the pond. The rest of the day, they spent sunning and preening themselves. Sometimes they dozed.

Preening is very important. Feathers must be kept free of dirt. Lice can live in the feathers. Preening helps to get rid of the lice. Swans and other birds use their bills like combs.

Swans have over 25,000 feathers on their bodies. That's more than any other bird. Every year, many of their feathers fall out. This is called *molting*. New feathers grow back in their place.

Birds have four kinds of feathers. Down feathers are very soft. They lie close to the birds' bodies. Birds also have body feathers, wing feathers, and tail feathers.

Chapter 3

The sun was up! The pond was alive with sound. Red-winged blackbirds sang from their nests in the reeds. Fish jumped and fed on insects flying over the water. Ducks nesting at the edge of the pond quacked loudly.

Daphne and her mate stood up. They stretched their legs and long necks. They ruffled their feathers. Then together, they slid into the water. Around and around they paddled. Swans have large webbed feet that help them paddle in the water.

The pair fed on plants and grasses. After they ate their fill, they went back to their island. They shook themselves dry. They preened themselves. Then they preened each other.

Daphne and her mate rubbed their necks together. Swans show a lot of affection. A cob will fight to his death to protect his mate and cygnets.

It was time to get back to nest building. The cob swam to the far shore. With his bill, he plucked twigs and grasses. Then he swam back to his mate.

He tossed the twigs and grasses over his
back. They landed on the ground near
Daphne.

The pen sat in the middle of her nest.
Carefully, she pushed the twigs and grasses
down around her body. She wiggled back and
forth to make a hollow spot. For hours, the
two worked hard.

Then it was time to eat. They spied some choice plants growing along the shore. The swans made their way to them. They fed on the juicy plants.

When the cob was full, he began to clean his feathers. Suddenly, he jumped. He had heard a sound. He jerked his head toward it.

A pair of geese was circling the pond. They were looking for a nesting site. The geese landed on the muskrat house.

The cob began to beat his wings. Half running, half flying, he made his way toward the strangers.

The cob hissed at the male goose. The gander hissed back. The female goose slipped quietly into the water. She swam a few feet away.

Daphne swam toward the female. She made low hissing sounds at the goose. The female goose hissed right back. But she moved farther away.

The cob snorted angrily. The mad gander honked loudly. They beat their wings at each other. Suddenly, the cob latched onto the gander's neck with his bill. It closed down harder and harder.

The gander squawked loudly. At last he broke free. The geese flew away. They decided to look for another nesting site.

Swans do not mind ducks nesting on the same pond. But they do not want geese or other swans nearby. Swans usually nest at least a half mile apart from one another.

It's not always easy for waterfowl to find good nesting sites. Much of the wetlands has been filled in. Humans use the land for farming and building houses.

Also, sprays have been used to kill insects and vegetation in and around wetlands. This keeps waterbirds from nesting. In recent years, more and more habitat has been lost.

Years ago, there were thousands of swans. The American Indians hunted only enough swans to fill their needs. Meat was eaten. Wing bones were carved into beads. And leg bones were shaped into sewing tools.

When the early settlers came, they also killed the swans for food. But they did so in much greater numbers.

Swans were killed for their skins and their down. Down is the covering of very soft feathers on the swan's body. It was used for powder puffs and pillow and bed stuffing. Hatmakers used the feathers for decorations.

By 1930, trumpeter swans were in danger of becoming extinct. In 1932, there were fewer than 100 trumpeter swans left in the world. Most of these lived in an area near Yellowstone National Park.

In 1935, the National Wildlife Refuge was established at Red Rock Lakes in Centennial Valley, Montana.

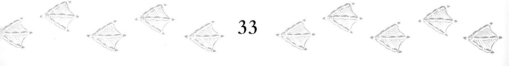

Over the years, some swans have been moved
from Red Rock Lakes. Placed in other wildlife
refuges, they have started new flocks.

Today there are about 16,000 trumpeter swans
in North America. About 13,000 live in Alaska
and spend their winters on the Pacific coast.
About 1,600 live in Canada. In the Midwest,
there are about 500. More than 500 live in
Idaho, Wyoming, and Montana. This includes
the flock at the Red Rock Lakes refuge.

Chapter 4

By the seventh day, the nest was a foot high. It takes a lot of grasses and plants to build such a large nest. But it was not finished.

Daphne and her mate spent as much time doing nothing as they did working on their nest. They enjoyed sunning themselves on the bank. And they enjoyed preening themselves.

Several times a day, they flew around the pond area. They needed to exercise their wings.

There were baby ducks on the pond. But their parents were careful to keep them away from the swans' island.

Baby muskrats were just leaving their den. Daphne kept a close watch on the muskrat family. And she kept a close watch on a mink

that came to the pond. The mink made
Daphne and her mate nervous.

Although minks are quite small, they will
attack almost any animal. It doesn't matter
how large. And they will eat almost anything.

Minks are very good swimmers. But they
don't like to swim in deep water. And the
swans' island was in deep water.

The mink was not interested in Daphne and her mate. It had its eye on the young muskrats. But it didn't want to swim out to the muskrat house.

So the mink waited in the reeds in the shallow water. It didn't have to wait long. A young muskrat swam too far away from its den. It became the mink's breakfast.

One day, Daphne woke from a nap in the sun to find a turtle napping beside her. The cob was swimming on the pond. Daphne jumped to her feet, hissing. She flapped her wings wildly. She pecked the turtle's shell sharply with her bill.

The poor turtle moved as fast as it could. It crawled straight into the water. It probably wondered what had just happened to it.

There were lots of animals that lived in and around the pond. Daphne and the cob paid little attention to them. They just made sure that none came too close to their nest.

One morning, Daphne saw something she had never seen before. Something came out of the woods not far from the pond. It crossed an open meadow. It came closer and closer.

When it got to the edge of the pond, it stood on its hind legs. It looked all around. Then it dropped down on all four feet. It drank from the pond.

The huge, black animal lumbered back across the meadow and into the woods. Daphne watched in awe. It was the first bear she had ever seen.

At last, the nest was finished. The cob and pen had worked on it for nearly two weeks. The nest was about 18 inches high and nearly 7 feet across.

It was lined with moss. Daphne had plucked soft feathers from her breast. Then she had added them to the moss.

There was a strange new feeling inside Daphne. The feeling told her it was time to lay her eggs. It was time to start her family.

The next morning, Daphne laid her first egg. It was creamy white. It was about twice the size of a chicken's egg.

A baby swan would grow inside the egg. It would grow for about 35 days. Then it would hatch.

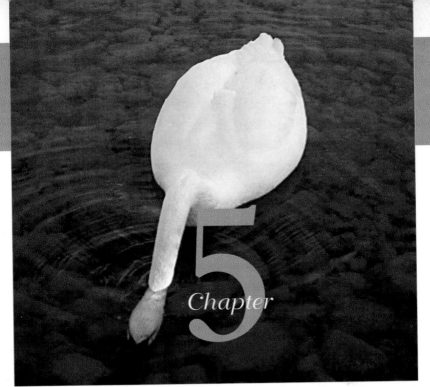

Chapter 5

Two days later, Daphne laid another egg. Now she only left her nest to eat and exercise. Her mate was always nearby.

By the end of the week, there were four eggs in the nest.

Daphne had been sitting on the nest for over two weeks. She was very tired. She had even lost a little weight. Her feathers drooped.

One afternoon, Daphne got off her nest. She stretched and ruffled her feathers. She slipped into the water with her mate. She began to feed hungrily.

A gentle breeze usually blew across the pond. But now it grew stronger and stronger. A dark cloud covered the sun. The whole sky turned black. Streaks of lightning flashed. Thunder rolled. Drops of rain fell.

All around the pond, animals scurried for cover. All but the frogs left. They loved the rain.

Small animals went down into their burrows. The muskrat family swam into their den. Turtles tucked themselves inside their

shells. Birds flew into thickets and fluffed up their feathers.

By the time Daphne got back to her nest, the storm was raging. Big raindrops pounded her head. Lightning lit the dark sky.

Daphne covered the eggs with her body. She spread her wings and lowered her head. With each roll of thunder, she trembled.

Her mate hovered nearby. Now and then, he reached out and touched her bill with his. He made soft cooing sounds deep in his throat. He seemed to say, "Don't worry. I'll protect you."

Daphne cooed back.

The storm raged on and on. Branches of willows and birches blew into the pond. It stormed late into the night.

A tree blew over. It hit the ground. The sound rumbled through the air.

The cob stretched out his neck and bugled. "KO-HO! KO-HO! KO-HO!"

Even over the roar of the wind and thunder, the swan's haunting call could be heard.

Just after midnight, the storm ended. It stopped as suddenly as it had begun. A steady drip, drip, drip fell from the trees' water-soaked limbs.

On day 35, the first cygnet hatched. He had an egg tooth on the tip of his upper beak. The baby used it to break open the shell.

Daphne preened his wet feathers. When he was dry, she pushed him under her body with the eggs. She had to keep her baby warm for a while.

During the next three days, the other three eggs hatched. All together, there were two males and two females. They were covered with soft gray feathers. They each weighed about eight ounces.

Daphne led her new family into the pond. The cygnets followed their mother. They paddled their little feet as hard as they could. Their father stayed nearby. He was ready to defend his family.

The cygnets pecked at insects that floated on the water. They watched their mother and father dip into the water and bring up plants. The cygnets tried too. But their necks were not long enough yet. For a while, they would feed on only insects and snails.

When the cygnets got tired, they climbed onto Daphne's back. It was a good place to ride. Sometimes they even napped while riding.

One day, the cygnets were swimming together. One of the males saw an insect fly by. He gave chase. The insect flew away. The cygnet turned back toward his parents. But he never made it.

An otter swam silently under the surface of the pond. It quickly snatched the baby swan and swam to shore.

For a long time, Daphne and the cob swam around the pond. They called for their baby. They were frantic. Where was he?

Finally, Daphne called the other cygnets to her. They climbed onto her back. She carried them to the island. Then she spread her wings. And the little ones nestled under them.

Daphne hung her head and sat very still.

Chapter 6

The three cygnets grew very fast. By the
time they were six weeks old, their soft down
was gone. They had many real feathers now.
They no longer ate only insects and snails.
They fed on water plants just as their parents
did.

The days were long and sometimes hot.
Daphne and her mate molted. They lost
many of their feathers.

When large birds molt, it is difficult to fly. They need their wing feathers to hold them up.

Spring flowers were losing their petals and summer flowers were blooming. On the pond, water lilies were in full bloom. The water level of the pond had dropped a little.

The swans spent much of their time on the bank. On hot days, they moved around as little as possible. But in the cool mornings and evenings, the cygnets played just as most young animals do.

On the water, they chased one another around and around. Sometimes they pulled one another's tail feathers. This made them squawk loudly.

One hot afternoon, Daphne was dozing in the shade of a willow tree. Her mate was nearby preening his molting feathers.

Suddenly, the cries of a cygnet woke Daphne. At once, she was on her feet.

The cygnet lay on her side. Something was wound around her legs. The cygnet struggled frantically. She tried to break free.

The baby swan was tangled in fishing line. The line had been left at the water's edge.

The cygnet's pitiful cries rang out. Daphne and her mate also cried as they fluttered around their baby.

They were frantic. They didn't know what to do. If the cygnet were threatened by an animal, her parents could help. But this was something new.

The young cygnet flopped about on the ground. Her parents and siblings clustered around. They watched in wonder and fear.

What was wrong? What had happened to the young swan to make her cry so? Why couldn't she get to her feet?

The cob began to peck at the fishing line. He attacked it like an enemy. Some of it came loose.

The cygnet continued to struggle. She tried and tried to get to her feet. After much more struggling, the cygnet was finally free.

The young swan had been very lucky. Many animals are not so lucky. Thoughtless people leave fishing lines and hooks around rivers and lakes. They discard plastic six-pack holders and other debris. These things can be very harmful to wildlife. Animals get caught in the lines and holders. Some even swallow hooks and other harmful trash.

At ten weeks, the three cygnets were half as large as their parents. They had all their feathers. But they were still gray. They would not be all white until their second winter.

The days were growing shorter and cooler. Leaves were changing from green to gold and red.

Many plants dried up. Their seeds fell to the ground. Or they blew in the wind. In the spring, they would sprout and new plants would grow.

Pond snails moved about more slowly. They spent more time in deeper water. It was warmer there.

Many songbirds and insects had left.

One morning when the swan family awoke, there was a thin layer of ice on the water's edge. And very little food was left for the swans to eat.

It was time to leave the pond and move south. The swans would spend the winter feeding in farmers' fields and in valley marshes.

But in the spring, Daphne and her mate would return to the pond. They would raise another family. And maybe they would use the same nest where their first cygnets had been born.

For more information, contact

Red Rock Lakes NWR
Monida Star Route, Box 15
Lima, MT 59739

email: r6rw_rrl@mail.fws.gov
phone: (406) 276-3536
fax: (406) 276-3638